MW00574776

CONTEMPORARY AMERICAN EROTIC PHOTOGRAPHY

MELROSE

CONTEMPORARY AMERICAN EROTIC PHOTOGRAPHY

Volume I

**JOYCE BARONIO·CHRIS CALLIS·PHILLIP DIXON
JEFF DUNAS·ROBERT FARBER·LARRY DALE GORDON
MITCHEL GRAY·ART KANE·ANTONIN KRATOCHVIL
STAN MALINOWSKI·ROBERT MAPPLETHORPE
KEN MARCUS·RICHARD NOBLE·PETER STRONGWATER**

There have been numerous compilation style books of photography and in particular, erotic photography, published in recent years. They have been characterized by collections of a variety of different photographer's portfolios. « CONTEMPORARY AMERICAN EROTIC PHOTOGRAPHY » differs from these other books in several important ways. To begin with, each of the fourteen photographers included in this volume live and work in the United States. In addition, with few exceptions, the work included here has not been previously published. We have endeavored to publish a selection of work from each photographer where each was given the possibility of selecting their images for publication, and they were encouraged to contribute to the design of their respective portfolios. What makes this so interesting is the fact that for many of the photographers, this represented their first opportunity to participate in the final selection process and the fashion in which their photographs were presented. As we gave each photographer complete freedom in terms of what he or she held to be erotic, a new definition of contemporary erotic photography was likely to emerge.

Another unique aspect of this book is the fact that each of the images published here are available in limited editions of signed and numbered original prints for collector's, making the images available to a considerably larger audience than heretofore afforded photographers. In the past, there has never been a means of acquiring original photographs from these or other photographers except through galleries, and in general, galleries exhibit material for only a limit period and are normally situated in major cities only. All one needs to do is write in care of the publisher and request that a price list be sent. This will list each photograph by page and its price and available sizes. Each print will be printed either by the photographers themselves or under their direct supervision. Photography is an art which lends itself to exposure before the masses as no other art medium has before. People from the world over can now participate in the acquisition of photography by a relatively simple procedure.

« CONTEMPORARY AMERICAN EROTIC PHOTOGRAPHY » will be published with regular frequency, affording photographers a medium to present their personal and/or professional erotic experimentation. This will provide those interested to assemble a collection of the best of the contemporary work being produced on a continuing basis by the frontrunners of American photographic erotica. Also planned is a sister version entitled « Masters of European Erotic Photography ». This title will be published in alternating seasons with the American version. We hope, therefore to establish a worldwide laboratory of serious erotic exploration by today's finest photographers.

The editors of this project had no way of knowing what form this book would take in its final presentation. We did know, however, that when all was said and done, we would be publishing a book which respected the artistic integrity of each of the photographers invited. We deliberately selected photographers whose orientation was photographing women but not necessarily those who specialize in erotica. We felt that in the final analysis this would yield a broader, fresher range of work. The combination of superior technique and lack of stereotyped images has contributed to making « CONTEMPORARY AMERICAN EROTIC PHOTOGRAPHY » a true departure from the expected.

As a way of illustrating the diversity of the photographers who have participated in this first volume, we have only to glance at the list of contributors. JOYCE BARONIO is primarily a fine art photographer whose backround includes teaching select groups of students in private workshops. She is the author of a highly acclaimed book entitled « 42nd Street Studio ». CHRIS CALLIS operates a successful fashion and beauty studio in New York. He first came to prominence in the early seventies in the now defunct « Viva » magazine which launched many of today's top photographers under the art direction of Rowan Johnson. During the seventies, PHILLIP DIXON was known as the most contemporary of Playboy's photographers. In 1978 he left to start a new career in fashion and beauty advertising. JEFF DUNAS is well known for his three highly acclaimed books, « Captured Women », « Mademoiselle, Mademoiselle ! » and « Voyeur ». These books have been well received worldwide. Himself the author of five books of photography, « Images of Women », « The Fashion Photographer », « Professional Fashion Photography », « Moods », and « Farber Nudes », ROBERT FARBER has firmly established himself in his field. LARRY DALE GORDON is just becoming well known to the public but has long been well regarded in the advertising business for his fine work on such campaigns as Marlboro, Salem and many others. His work with Image Bank is highly visable in over 20 countries. Best known for his book, « The Lingerie Book », fashion and beauty photographer MITCHEL GRAY's distinctive style is widely recognized. ART KANE is one of the giants of America's photographers. Having began his career at Look and Life in the sixties, he has emerged today as one of the world's top fashion and beauty photographers working for such magazines as Vogue and Harpers Bazaar. A new book, Art Kane : Paper Dolls, was recently published. Since 1974 ANTONIN KRATOCHVIL has been popular for his surreal and avant guarde photography. His work has appeared in Zoom, Photo, Vogue, Esquire, Playboy and Cosmopolitan. One of the world's most widely traveled fashion photographers, STAN MALINOWSKI started his career over twenty years ago and is known for his beautiful and sensual photography of women. Currently one of America's talked about artists, ROBERT MAPPLETHORPE's work is collected by major museums and has been exhibited in a vast number of the world's largest photo galleries. His book, « Lady Lisa Lyons », has sold extremely well. KEN MARCUS, a regular contributor to Playboy, is best known for having photographed the last five Playboy calendars. He conducts lectures and workshops in photographing women and gives seminars to a wide range of interested groups. Known in the advertising community as one of the most important and prolific of the advertising photographers in Los Angeles, RICHARD NOBLE has created countless national campaigns. PETER STRONGWATER is a photographer wearing a multitude of hats. He is the Project Director of the United States Information Agency's on-going project of photographing Americans who have changed the world in which we live. In addition, he has been a major contributor to Andy Warhol's Interview since its inception and has created many of its most memorable covers and photographs.

*E*ach photographer included in this work explains the techniques employed in the making of their images and discribes his or her own feelings on erotic photography in a special section following the photographs.

*W*e hope you will enjoy this edition of « CONTEMPORARY AMERICAN EROTIC PHOTOGRAPHY » and look forward to planning future editions with these and other fine photographers.

The Editors.

THE PHOTOGRAPHS

JOYCE **BARONIO**

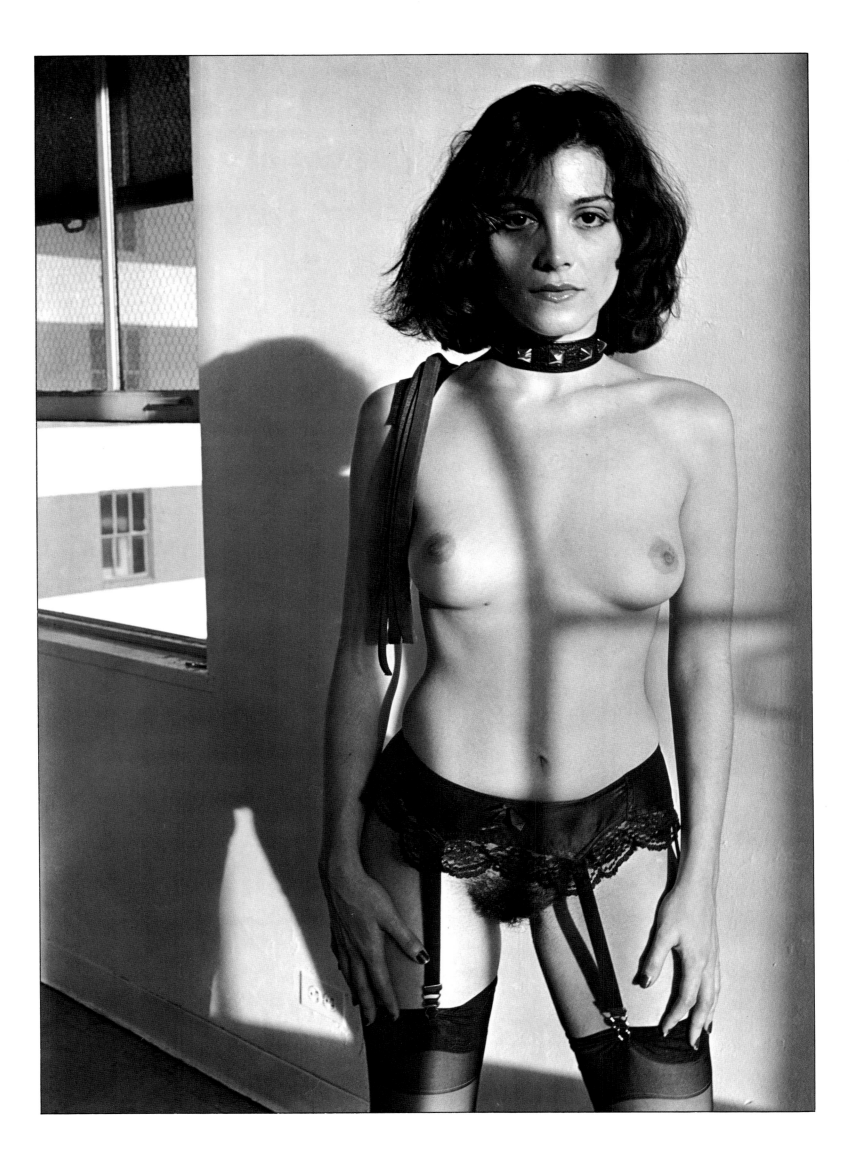

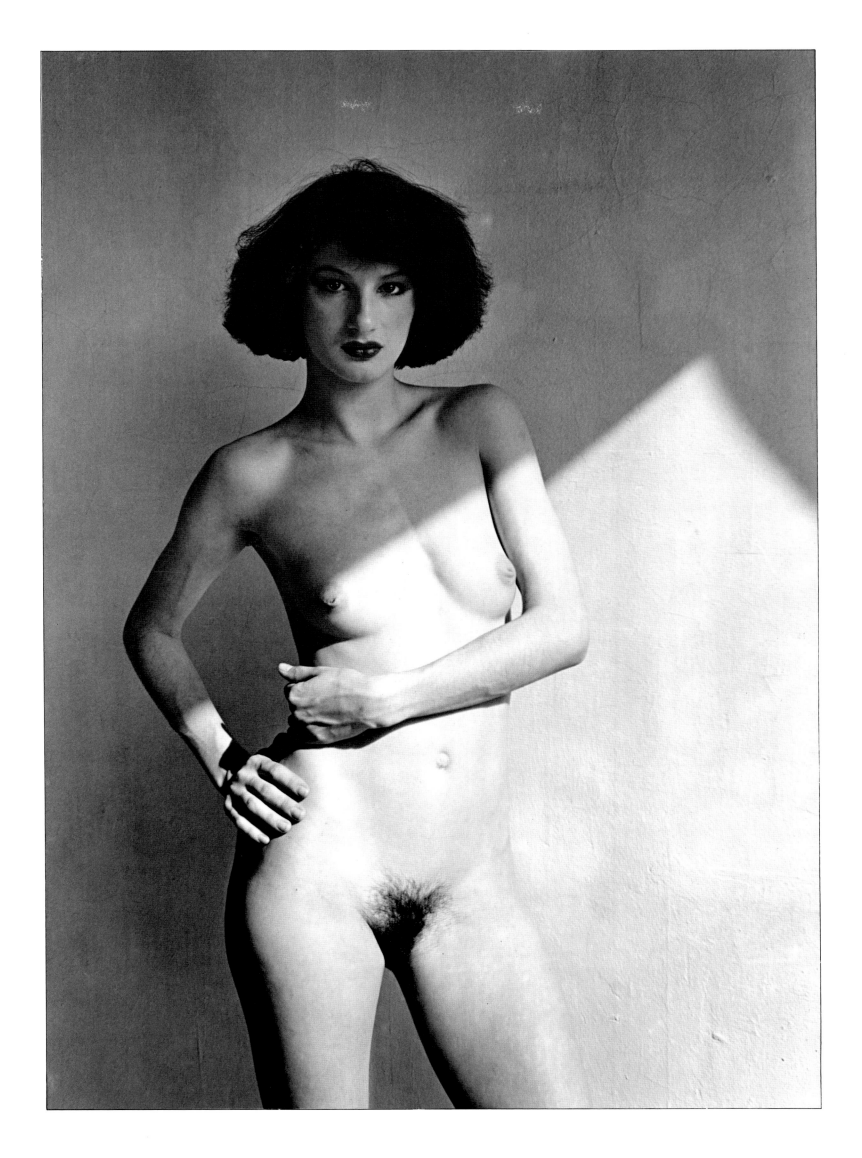

CHRIS **CALLIS**

PHILLIP **DIXON**

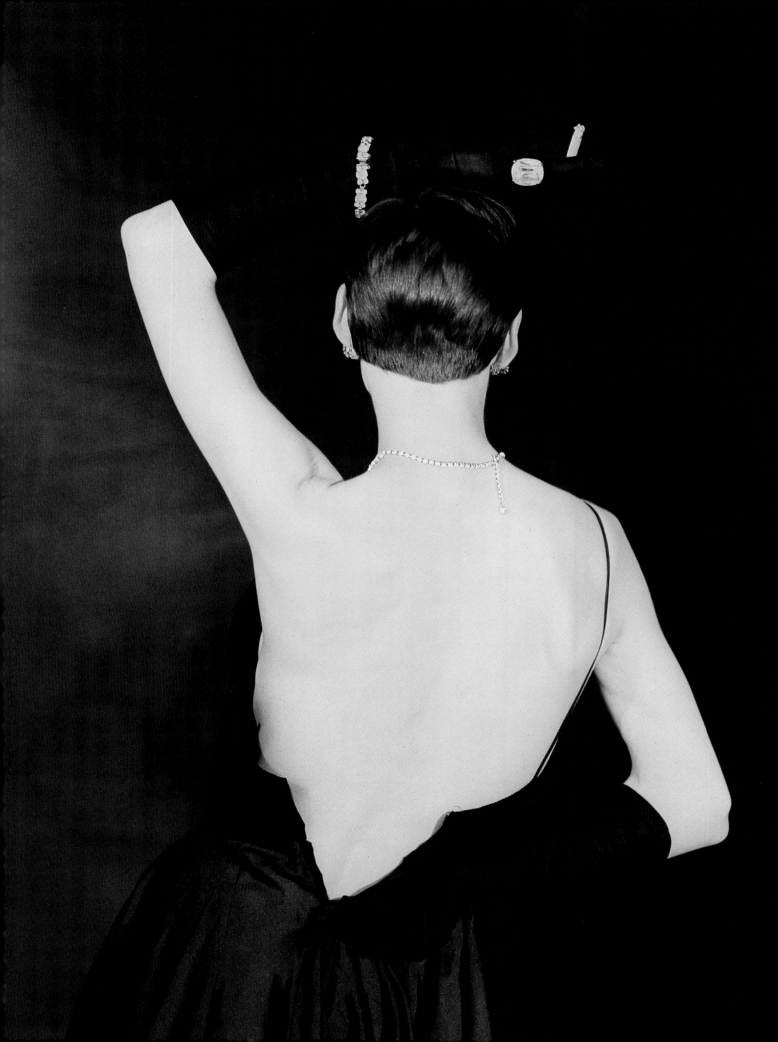

JEFF DUNAS

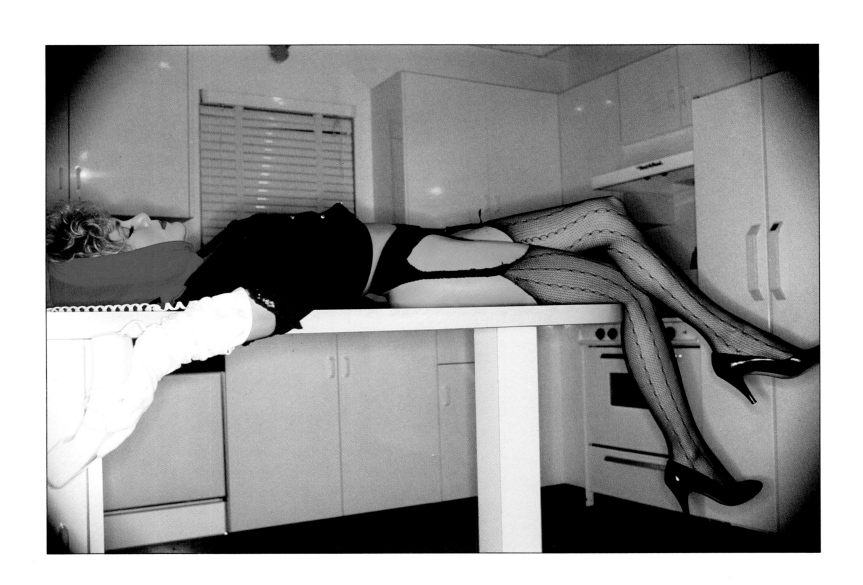

ROBERT **FARBER**

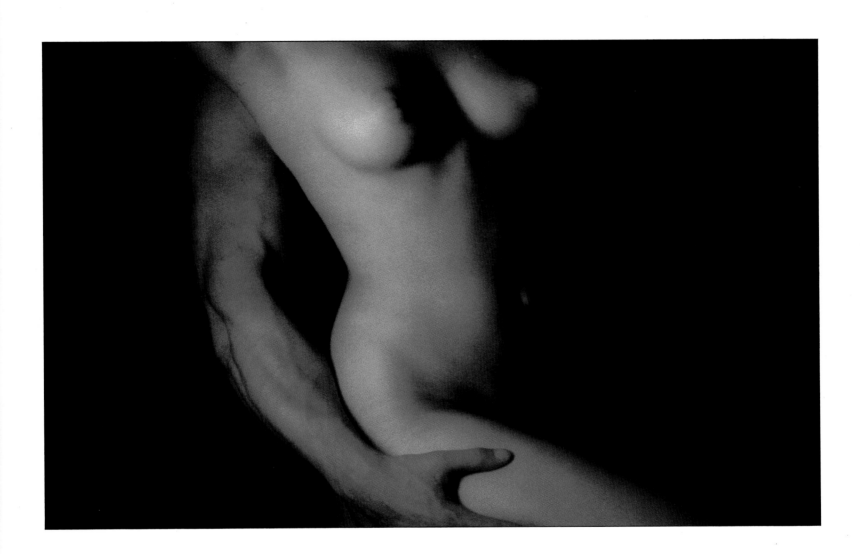

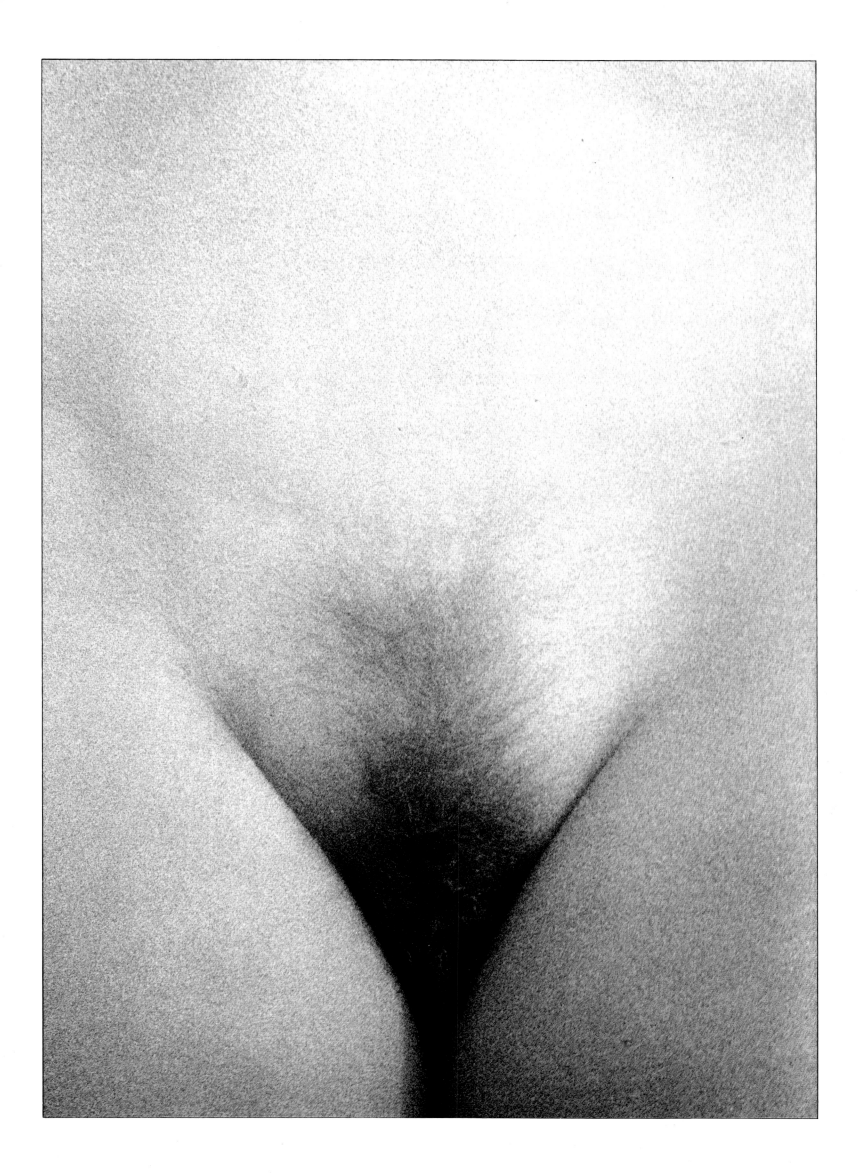

LARRY **DALE GORDON**

MITCHEL **GRAY**

ART **KANE**

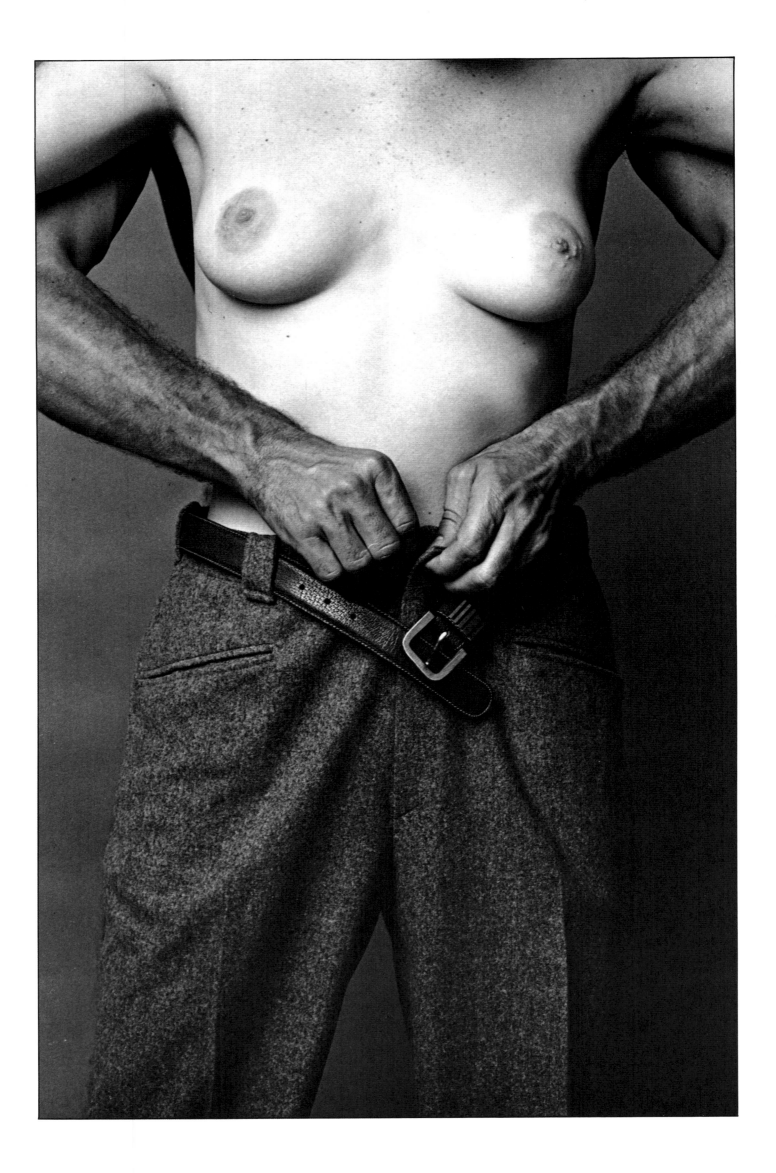

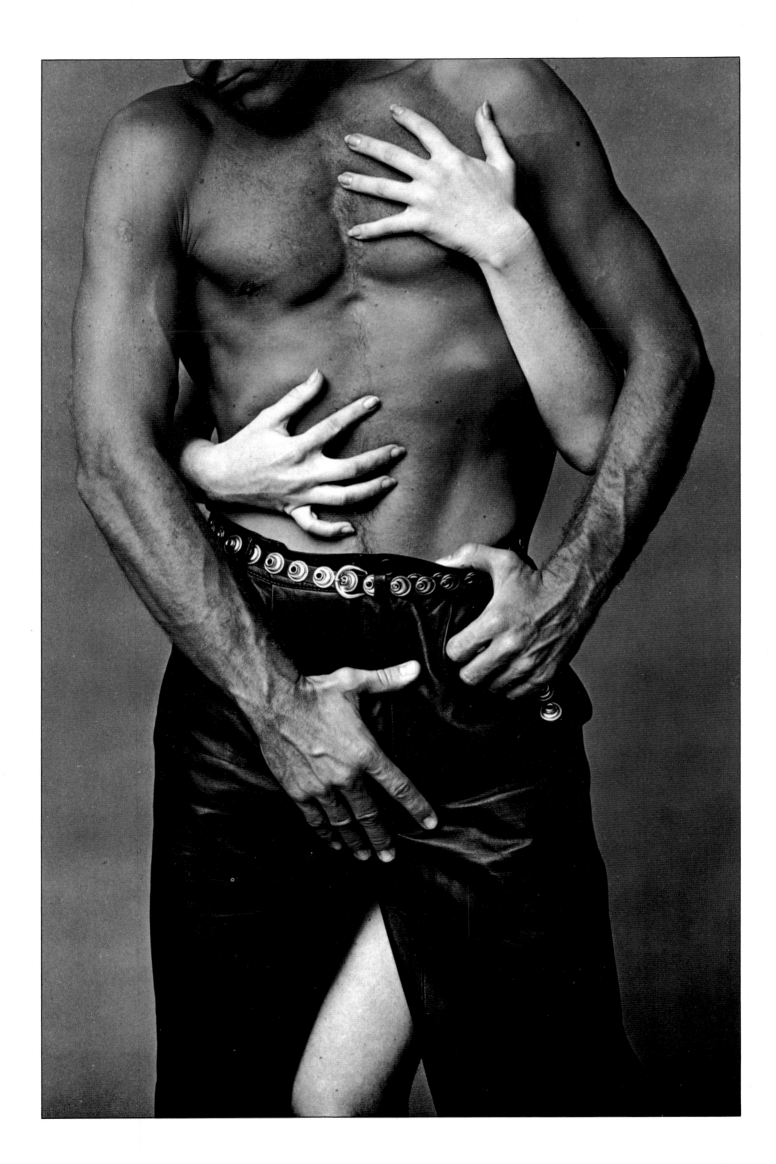

ANTONIN **KRATOCHVIL**

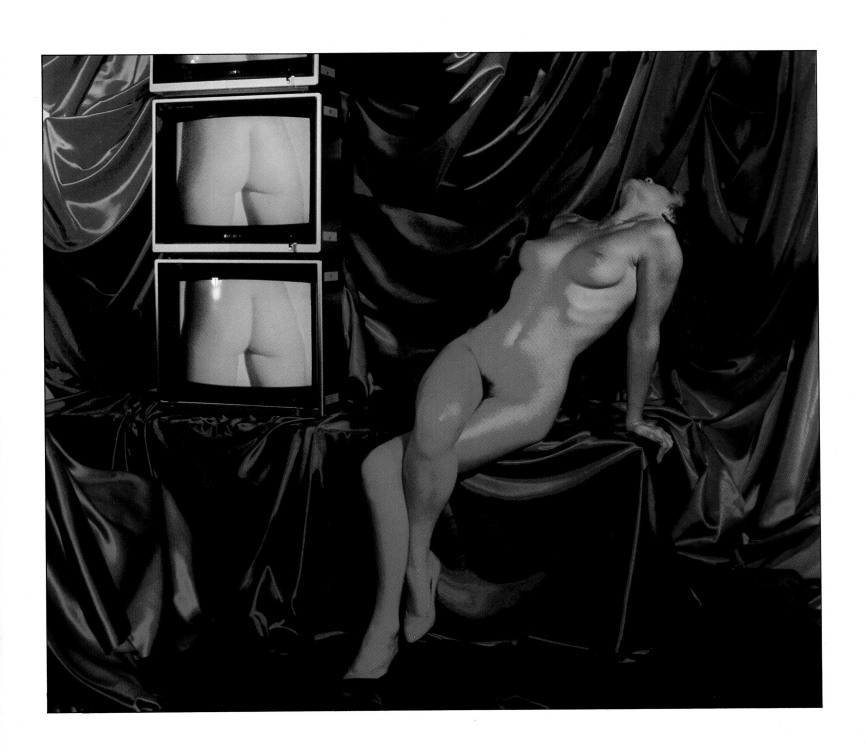

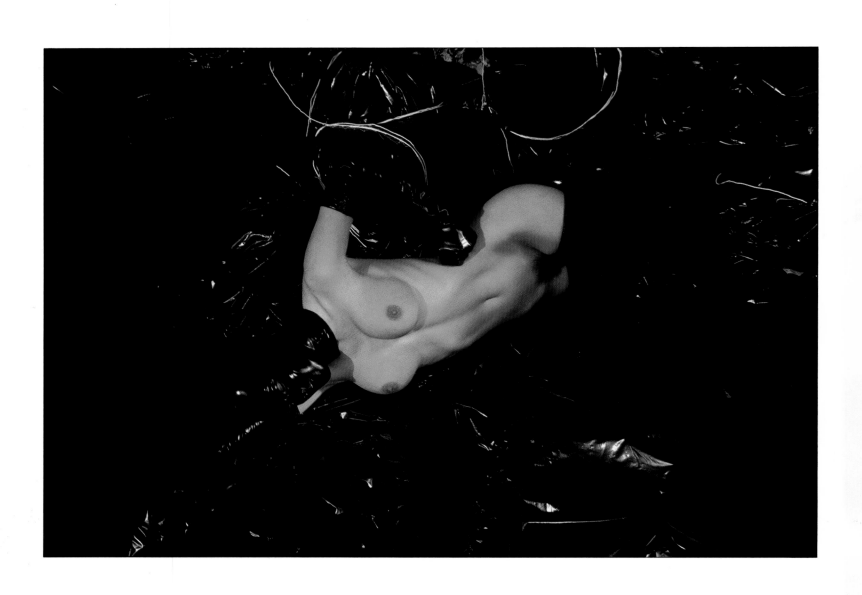

STAN **MALINOWSKI**

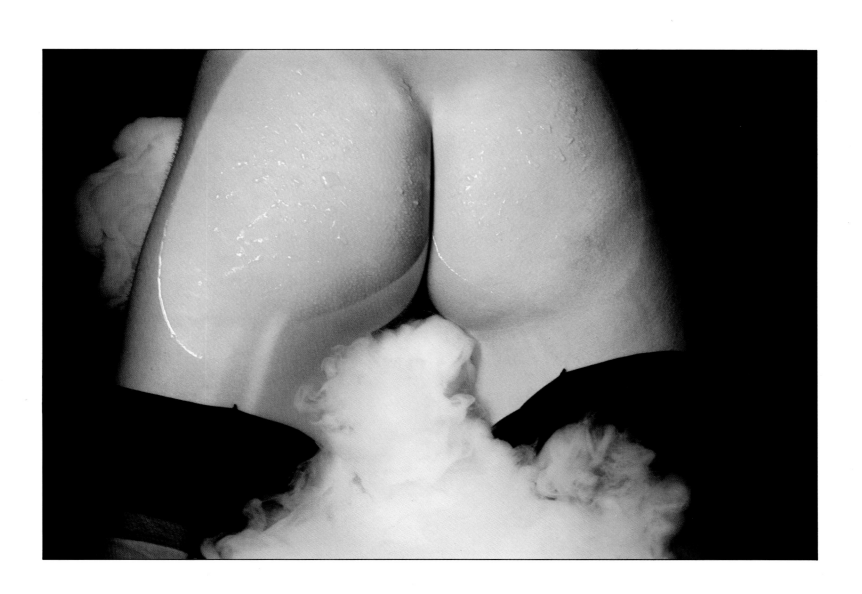

ROBERT **MAPPLETHORPE**

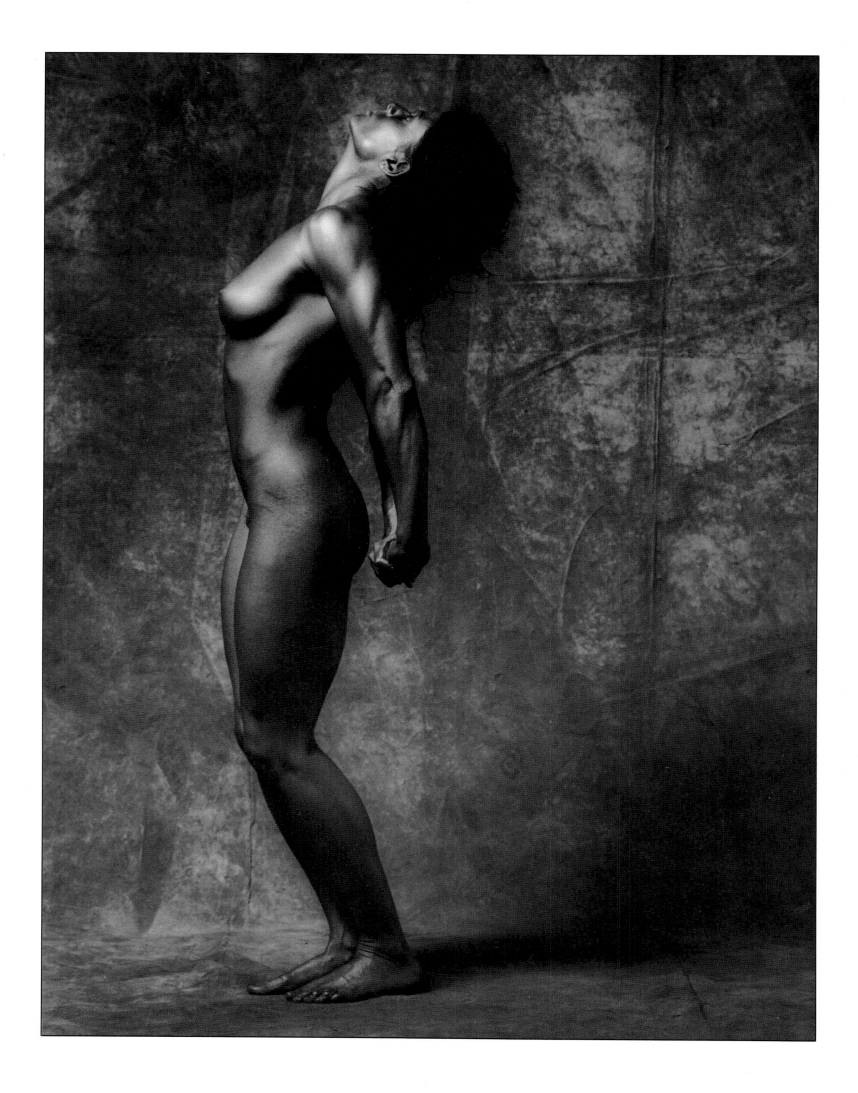

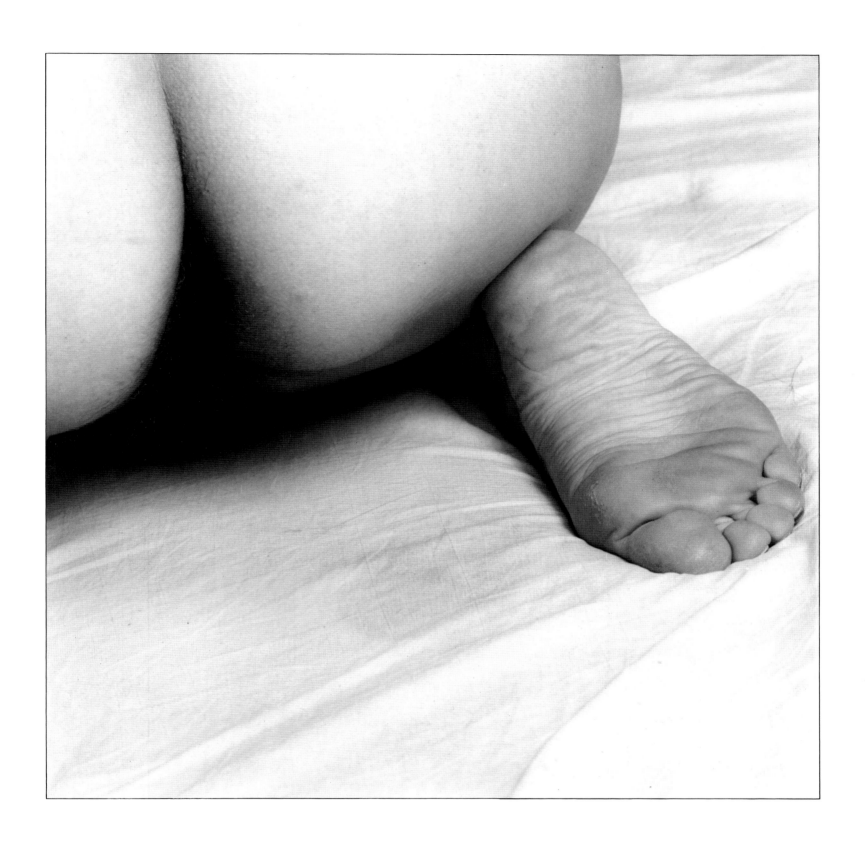

KEN MARCUS

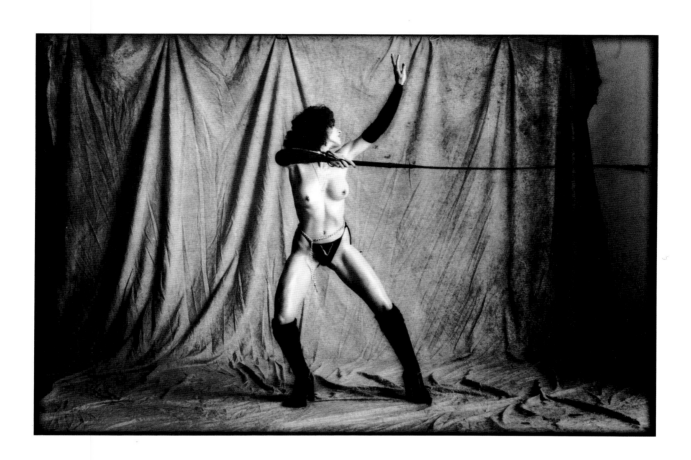

RICHARD **NOBLE**

PETER **STRONGWATER**

THE PHOTOGRAPHERS

Joyce Baronio attended the University of New Mexico, the University of Illinois, Kenyon College, and received her Masters of Fine Arts degree at Yale University where she studied under the legendary Walker Evans. She has made numerous exhibitions and has had portfolios published in dozens of magazines worldwide including MS., New York Magazine, the British Journal of Photography, G.Q. and American Photographer.

Her book, « 42nd Street Studio » was published by Pyxidium Press in 1980. It was through this book that her work became well known in the international photography community. Her photography is in the collections of the Yale University Art Gallery, la Bibliothèque Nationale of Paris and Norton's Museum of Art. She is currently the coordinator of the graduate program in photography at the Maryland Institute of Art in Baltimore.

JOYCE BARONIO

« The notion of « erotic photography » is basically nonsensical. Eroticism is the word we use to define our own complex response to a photograph. And I do not think that our responses can be categorized so neatly. One can, of course, have erotic subject matter or content. In my work, I try to distribute the content equally over the entire surface of the print. My subject matter is not contained in a part of the work, but covers the whole surface. In this way, the whole picture has equal weight and life. »

For the photos from « 42nd Street Studio », Baronio used a Pentax 6 × 7 camera with the 75mm lens. For the others, she used an old Rolleiflex with a Schneider Lens, also 75mm. For both series, the technique was the same; the film is initially overexposed, then underdeveloped as much as possible, about 5 minutes. There is also two water baths before and after developer — the first with a wetting solution to prevent streaking, and the second in plain water for more detail in the shadow areas. « It is essential to remember that I work only on sunny days, so I'm shooting in bright sunlight. The exposures are usually 1/4 to 1/15th of a second at F 16. My aim is to make prints in which tones remain on the surface of the print — gradations of grey are my delight. »

CHRIS CALLIS

Born in Yreka, California, Chris Callis attended the University of California at Davis, where he received a B.S. in food science. While at the university, Callis began a love affair with photography. He subscribed to the "Famous Photographers Correspondance School" with an eye to pursuing photography as a career. His decision to specialize in fashion photography came about after seeing "Blow up" in 1968. That same year, he was drafted into the army and worked at Fort Sill, Oklahoma and later Vietnam as an army photographer. After his tour of duty, he attended the Art College of Design in Los Angeles. Since 1974 he has been living and working in New York and has become well known for his innovative incorporations of movement and light.

"The series started when I first photographed a friend of mine who wore a sheer antique dress through which you could see her "derrière". Everyone who saw the photograph wanted a print, so I continued the series with the idea in mind that the nudity you see is almost accidental. I think the philosophy that "less is more" is what I like in erotic photography."

The photographs were made in black and white, with Plus-X film rated at ASA 64. The film was then overdeveloped 15 percent, printed on Portriga Rapid F (glossy surface) and hand colored.

 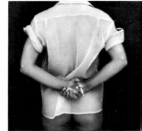  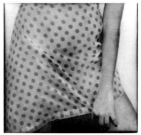 

Born and raised in Los Angeles, Phillip Dixon began his career in photography at the age of 19, when he began working at Playboy. He quickly earned himself a reputation as a photographer of distinctive images of women.

Feeling that the viewpoint of women as reflected at Playboy was considerably different than his own, he left Playboy in 1978 to begin a new career in fashion and beauty advertising. He currently lives and works in New York City.

PHILLIP DIXON

« For me, the eye of the beholder defines eroticism. The women I photograph have to be beautiful in all respects, not simply physically beautiful. For me, the back of a neck, the side of a breast, the tilt of a head are more suggestive of eroticism than a woman fully nude. This applies in photography as well as in life. »

Phillip Dixon works exclusively with the Pentax 6×7 and Pentax lenses. His favorite lens is the 165 mm f 2.8. He prefers working with tungsten lights vrs. strobe.

PHOTO 1. Pentax 6×7. Daylight. 200 mm f 4. lens. Made with EPR 120 film. Los Angeles studio, 1984.
PHOTO 2. Pentax 6×7. Combination tungsten and daylight. Normal lens. EPR 120 film. Los Angeles studio, 1984.
PHOTO 3. Pentax 6×7. Tungsten light. Normal lens. EPR 120 film. Los Angeles studio, 1984.
PHOTO 4. Pentax 6×7. Combination daylight and tungsten. Los Angeles studio, 1984.
PHOTO 5. Pentax 6×7. 165 mm f 2.8 lens. Combination daylight and tungsten. Los Angeles studio, 1984.
PHOTO 6 & 7. Pentax 35 mm camera with 105 mm lens. Video lights with type B Kodachrome. New York City, 1984.

Jeff Dunas is perhaps the only photographer featured in this book whose full time activity is the creation of erotic photography.

Born in Los Angeles, he began photography as a hobby at the age of 8. Living both in Paris and Los Angeles, he is the author of three books of photography; «Voyeur», «Mademoiselle, Mademoiselle!» and «Captured Women». In all, his books have sold over 185,000 copies worldwide. Portfolios of his work have appeared in such magazines as Photo, Zoom, Photo Magazine, Photo-Revue, Photo Reporter, Playboy, Amateur Photographer, One Woman, Amica, Harpers Bazaar Italia and L'Official Homme. His exhibitions have been presented in New York, Paris, Los Angeles, Chicago. Others are planned in London and Tokyo. His timeless and intriging images of women are a reflection of his distinctive style and technique.

JEFF DUNAS

«A woman's unique sensuality lies in her power to project subtle, almost indecernable nuances. I try to capture on film that special essence which is the fascination she holds for both men and women alike — that fleeting, revealing moment, — that private moment. It is imperative that a woman, clothed or unclothed, retain her dignity, her allure and her mystery. We can train ourselves, through exposure to high quality photography, films, and a sharpened perception in general, to see things of great erotic content, even in everyday situations. Erotic is a word which lies in the intellectual perception of life. It exists only in the mind and is completely different for each person. My images are reconstructions of moments I have seen and experienced in life.»

Jeff Dunas works exclusively with the Mamiya RZ-67 camera and the Mamiya RZ lenses. «Because my photographs are destined primarily for exhibition and publication, I find the 6 × 7 format ideal for high quality image detail and ease of use.» He uses Ektachrome film and prefers 220 to 120. His electronic flash equipment is all made by Balcar.

PHOTO 1. RZ-67, strobe light Malibu Beach, 1984. Ektachrome 64.
PHOTO 2. RZ-67, strobe light mixed with daylight. Malibu Beach, 1984. Ektachrome 64.
PHOTO 3. RZ-67, daylight mixed with tungsten. New York Studio, 1984.
PHOTO 4. Exceptionally, this was made on 35 mm, using Kodachrome 64 and strobe light. Nemours, France 1983.

All images except number 4 were processed by the A & I Color Laboratory in Los Angeles. Photo 4 was processed by Central Color, Paris.

ROBERT FARBER

Born in New Jersey, Robert Farber has lived and worked in New York since he began his career. In contrast to many other photographers, Farber's first public exposure came through « fine art » galleries rather than through commercial channels. His work has been exhibited widely in the United States and Europe. He is the author of five successful books, « Images of Women », « Professional Fashion Photography », « Moods », « The Fashion Photographer » and his most recent, « Farber Nudes ». (All available through Amphoto). He is currently at work on a book to be edited by Jacqueline Onassis for Doubleday entitled « By the Sea ». Farber enjoys a career in advertising and fashion photography as well, and regularly works for such clients as Bloomingdales, Paco Rabanne, Revlon and others.

« If I were to make any type of generalization about these photographs at all, it's that in each, I've tried to capture a sense of wholeness; in the same way that faces can be distracting in a full-body photograph, so can certain parts of the body. There were times when I felt I had to de-emphasize breasts, thighs or buttocks. There's always an erotic temptation to focus on a particularly appealing «part», but that kind of objectification just isn't compatible with the sense of the human form I'm after in these pictures. Bodies are fully as expressive as faces. Sometimes the arch of a back, the curve described by an arm, the tension of an outstreched leg can evoke responses that a facial expression can't. »

« The line between the erotic and the pornographic has to do with just this : pornography is disembodied from any sense of a whole human being ; the erotic allows that wholeness to exist. If some of these pictures are erotic, it's an unashamed eroticism - something I'm happy spontaneously occurs. »

Robert Farber uses Minolta cameras and lenses and Agfa film and paper. His preference in electronic flash is for Balcar.

PHOTO 1. Daylight film, incandescent light.
PHOTO 2. Daylight. Minolta X700 with Minolta 35-105 zoom. Agfachrome 200 pushed to 400 ASA. 81-A filter with diffuser.
PHOTO 3. New York Studio. One light head (Balcar) above model. Agfachrome 200 pushed to 400.
PHOTO 4. Male nude. Window light. Agfa 400 black and white film pushed to 1600. Film developed in Rodinal developer.
PHOTO 5. Balcar softbox above model. Minolta 50 mm lens. Black and white Agfa film ASA 100.
PHOTO 6. Daylight. Minolta zoom lens. 35-105mm. Agfa black and white film pushed to 1600 ASA.
PHOTO 7. Balcar Strobe with grid spot. Printed on Portriga Number 3.

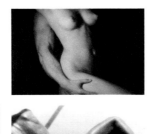

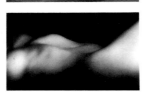
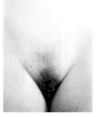

Larry Dale Gordon has traveled and worked in over 60 countries in his career as a photographer. He has lived in London, Rome and other European capitals but calls Los Angeles home. Fully at home with illustration, people, cars, and beauty, he is an extremely versatile photographer. He is now moving his portfolio towards beauty and fashion, and directing commercials for television. His client list includes American Motors, American Telephone and Telegraph, Coca Cola, Datsun, Hertz, Kent, Kodak, Life, Maybelline, Monsanto, Nabisco, Newsweek, Salem, Time, Town and Country and Vogue.

LARRY DALE GORDON

« Eroticism can be many things; a soft touch, a kiss, a word, a vision... anything in the eye of the beholder. The female form in itself is to me the most exciting form of eroticism. One of the most erotic photographs I have ever seen was done by Art Kane; it was a close shot of a woman's neck and shoulder. It was abstract and graphic, but so lovely and so sensual and so understated. Most interesting was the comparison of other photographer's interpretations of the erotic in the same article. In my eyes there was nothing to compare; they were all overt and obvious, showing much more than was needed. I don't find my photographs used in this book erotic in the sense of the Webster's interpretation; « (B) abnormally insistant sexual passion. » They are sculptures of the finest form, in the context of natural elements. »

PHOTO 1. Los Angeles Studio. Nikon F3. 35mm Lens. Norman Strobes. Ceiling bounce with red gel in the foreground through umbrella. Acetate on window in backround with blue gel.
PHOTO 2. Los Angeles Studio. Nikon FM. 28mm lens with polarizer. Norman Strobes. Black lucite table with hot water piped in from outside. Red gels over light source. Slight underexposure to saturate color.
PHOTO 3. Same as for photo 2.
PHOTO 4. Los Angeles Studio. Nikon FM. 85 mm lens. Norman Strobes bounced off white flat.
PHOTO 5. Los Angeles Studio. Nikon FM. 105 mm lens. Backlit sunlight.
PHOTO 6. Cabo San Lucas, Baja California, Mexico. The wind here is the important element. Nikon F3. 28 mm lens with polarizer. Natural sunlight.

All photographs were made with Kodachrome 25 film.

Born in South Orange, New Jersey, Mitchel Gray was educated at the University of Virginia. After three and one half years as an English major, Mitchel decided to pursue a career in fashion photography. For the past 15 years, he has lived in New York City working for a multitude of American, Japanese and German clients. «The lingerie Book» was published by St. Martins Press in 1980 and has been translated into four languages with total copies in print now exceeding 100,000.

«The lingerie Book» has been adapted for television.

MITCHEL GRAY

« The basic guideline in my philosophy of photographing women is that the end product must be at least as appealing, if not more so, to women as it is to men. This tenet guarantees a certain taste level and type of eroticism that transcends gender boundaries, allowing me to touch as large an audience as possible ».

« Technically speaking, I pride myself on being capable of expressing any thought I have. This requires a basic mastery of every lighting system individually, and more important for myself, an ability to blend lighting systems. I love the simplicity of daylight and the complexity of a ten light set-up. Both of these are illustrated in the selection of photographs included here ».

Black lingerie series (photos 1, 2, 3). Made for German Vogue. Hasselblad camera, 150 mm lens. Tri-X, developed in D-76. Light source, daylight and reflectors.

White lingerie series (photos 4, 5, 6, 7). Hasselblad camera, square and horizontal formats. 150 mm lens. Tri-X, developed in D-76. Light source : Balcars, (approximately 10 heads, 5 power packs). Mixed spotlight and broad source strobe with tungsten added.

ART KANE

Art Kane is known internationally for his bold and sometimes startling photographic illustrations. Having studied under the legendary Alexi Brodovich in the early fifties, he soon was producing his unique images for Look, Life, Esquire and others. The receipient of a myriad of awards, many of them gold medals, he was presented with the distinguished « Lifetime Achievment Award » from the American Society of Magazine Photographers in 1984. Since its inception over

40 years ago, the only other receipients of this honor have been Edward Stiechen, Irving Penn, Phillip Halsman, Alfred Eisenstadt, Arnold Newman and Fritz Goro.

Art Kane emerged from the decline and subsequent demise of the Look and Life era as one of today's top fashion and advertising photographers working regularly for Italian Vogue, Geo, Stern, German Vogue and Harpers Bazaar.

« Several years ago, when I was immersed in a period of conscientious reading and soul searching, I came across a book entitled, quite simply, « He and She » (a study of male and female relationships, but more important — a study of the male and female within each and every one of us). It took but a few pages of the first volume for me to realize how little I had known about myself as a man and how equally sparse was my knowledge of the members of the opposite sex. »

« I had always accepted the fact that men were simply men and women simply women, never realizing that each and every male personality embodies both a male and a female counterpart. And for every female, of course, the same in reverse. The only difference lies in the proportions of the mix. Unless a proper balance, a genuine compatibility exists between the male and female within us, we shall never know the meaning of a peaceful, loving, and everlasting relationship with any member of the opposite sex. When a man denies or suppresses the female within, the result is usually an insensitive and overpowering machismo. When a woman denies or surpresses the male within, the result can often produce a false timidity and total dependance. »

« These photographs were taken purely as fashion photos for Italian Mens's Bazaar but I suppose as is so often the case in my editorial work, the pictures represent the visual manifestations of the many and varied ideas I have embraced while reading. It comes as no surprise to me that these photographs were shot only a few weeks after having read and thoroughly digested the books « He and She ».

The photographs were made in Art Kane's New York studio using Plus-X film, developed normal. Nikon camera with 105 mm lens. Dynalite strobes.

A native of Czechoslovakia, Antonin Kratochvil in a second generation photographer. His father, a photographer, maintained a studio in Prague. In the late sixties, he left Czechoslovakia to study photography in Amsterdam at the Gerrit Reitveld Art Academy. The circumstances surrounding his departure from Prague are vague and he rarely elaborates. After receiving his Bachelor of Fine Arts degree in 1972, he emigrated to the United States, settling in Los Angeles and later, New York, where he is presently a certified artist by the City of New York.

Publications such as Camera, Foto, Panorama, Photo, Photo Graphia Italiana, Picture Magazine, Photographie, Color Photo, Zoom, Photo-Revue, and Photo Italy have published his portfolios.
His work has also appeared in the following books ; Art in Photography, (Time/Life Books), Creative Camera Annual, and American Photography Today. He presently works in fashion and beauty for such magazines as Vogue, Playboy, Penthouse, Esquire, Cosmopolitan, Amica, Geo, New York Magazine and Rolling Stone.

ANTONIN KRATOCHVIL

Interview with Antonin Kratochvil by Bob Krcil.

BK : ''Antonin, when did you start taking your first erotic photographs ?''
AK : ''Well, I always... uh... When I was in Prague, as a youngster, we had a studio where we always took girls and photographed them nude. But then, it was only a pretext, you know... It was a PRETEXT. We used to get some lovely ladies and then see them nude and... eventually make love or something, you know, that sort of thing. So I set up a studio in my apartment and we had our orgies there, you know.''
BK : ''Photographic ones ?''
AK : ''Yes, of course !! We started with photos and ended up, uh, well,... It was fabulous !!''
BK : ''But when you work nowadays, do you have a certain concept ?''
AK : ''Yeah, I visualize, I see things... I make mental notes, and then I SEE things, you know, I get an idea. A loose one, a basis. And then I look for girls to play in it. And usually I sell my idea to a magazine who produces the piece.''
BK : ''As for these « mental notes », do you think it's your subconsious ?''
AK : ''Exactly. Yes, definately. Desires...''
BK : ''Photographic descriptions of desires ?''
AK : ''Yes, of my desires, although some pictures are not my desires. It's just the aesthetics, or breaking of the taboos. Something like that, you know. Being daring, experimental.''
BK : ''So in some way, you recreate what is inside you.''
AK : ''Well, actually I'm... I don't USE women as an... In my pictures I use women with respect... I don't try to understand this particular woman I'm photographing ; I'm trying to get her into my concept. I mean it's built around her but it's not necessarily HER. I'm trying to project what I see, which is sort of chauvinistic in a way but as an artist, you know, you have the right to do that. I see them purely as aesthetic forms which are acting in my plays, my movies. Because my photo sessions are like movies you know ? They have a beginning, a middle and an end ! It's not a single image, but a series of 10-15 pages I'm after ! I don't even KNOW if my photographs are erotic. I let others judge for themselves but eh, I don't find my photos erotic myself, you know... Well, the EROS is there... eh... it's more fantasies, it's more the... It's not as BLATANT, you know... It pisses me off

when someone say's ''Ah ! You do pornography... ! You know, I don't see myself as a pornographer at all. Because if I'm a pornographer, then Rubens was one. And every fucking painter who is glorified now, who ever painted a nude body is a fucking pornographer ! And I don't FEEL like a pornographer. I think that America is sort of twisted in that aspect. Everything is put into one catagory ; they don't define or recognize the differences... Because of their own insecurities, I'm sure. With SEX, America is, and always has been, eh... very UNEASY about sex.—Nudity.''
BK : ''Do you see a different approach in Europe, or France, specifically ?''
AK : ''Definately. More sophisticated and more acceptable. In Europe, you can see nudity even in T.V. commercials, which is UNBELIEVABLE !! It always shocks me when I come to Europe and I see, you know, nudes selling soap. Which is the way to do it !''
BK : ''So erotic photography is something you return to periodically. Do you persue other directions ?''
AK : ''I like to play games, you know ? I'm a child, you know ? I like to play games. I hate straight fucking... umm... there always has to be... eh... I need RENOIR !! I need a painting of Renoir and blind musicians, you know ? I can't make love in a cold corridor... I have aesthetic requirments and I'm definately an aesthetic. I just can't fuck like a proletarian, in a dark corner, you know what I'm saying ? Unless it's in an elevator or something . recently I made love in a laundry room and I loved the noises of the machines... The washing machines... !''
BK : ''Got any pictures ?''
AK : ''No. But I just fucked in the laundry room and it was BEAUTIFUL !! mean, I need a SENSE OF ADVENTURE. And it's the same with my photos. Because a lot of times I make pictures in unbelievable places, where I'm... eh... Twice I got arrested, for taking nude photos in Arizona in the desert for a series with cactuses... yeah, it was beautiful, man...
BK : ''Do you ever recreate your photos in reality, afterwards ?''
AK : ''You mean... ?? No I never do. When I photograph, I'm absorbed in the aesthetics of it and the technical aspects. And so I don't have the time to... you know... I'm completely disconnected... And I NEVER touch my models !!''

Antonin Kratochvil uses NIKON FE cameras, and the NIKKOR 28 mm, 35 mm, and 50 mm lenses. His choice for film is either Kodachrome 64 or Ektachrome 64. In the studio, he uses the Norman 2,000, and Balcar strobes. Outside he uses Norman 200-B's with reflectors (gold for the skin tones). He also uses color gels over the strobe-heads.

Born in 1936, a native of Chicago, Stan Malinowski bought his first camera, an Argus C3, in 1955. While attending college, he developed a passion for photography. During his service as a military policeman in the United States Army, he sold his first cover to Popular Photography. In 1962 he opened his first studio in Chicago and proceeded to sell over 300 album covers and several thousand retail fashion ads. In addition, he produced many covers and features for Playboy. In 1974, he suffered a complete reversal in his fortunes and went to see Bob Guccione at Penthouse .

His many covers and centerfolds for Penthouse led him to Rochelle Udell and Alexander Lieberman at Vogue. Since then (1976), Malinowski's client list reads like a Who's Who in the world of fashion and beauty photography.

Among the magazines carrying his pages are Vogue, Harpers Bazaar, Cosmopolitan and Photo. His advertising clients include Valentino, Fendi, Christian Dior, More cigarettes and Clinique. He does fashion catalogues for the likes of May Company, Macy's, Sak's Fifth Avenue and his favorite, Bullock's.

STAN MALINOWSKI

« When I originally picked up a camera, nearly thirty years ago, my intention was merely to be accepted into the company of attractive women. Very quickly, however, I developed a great appreciation for excellence, as I saw it, in photographing women. In considering that which lends eroticism to a photograph, I am inclined to think about the inherent necessity for commercialism in the context of the photos, at least if one feels the need to earn an income from the photographs (having never been independantly wealthy I confess to requiring such an income). »

« When I first photographed centerfold pictorials for Penthouse the young woman and I would go off to a Carribean island, the model would do her own hair and makeup, and the elements of wardrobe would include a combination of things she brought, and items I would borrow or buy. In the past few years, a ''team effort'' has emerged, in which one is accompanied by a stylist, a hairdresser, a makeup artist and a photographer's assistant. That which had been a very personal and intimate environment has become like a small movie production on location, and the trade off has been the loss of some feeling, spontanéity and vulnerability for a slick production line look, of perhaps greater ''perfection'' but one of lesser sensitivity. »

« Virtually all my work now falls under the catagory of fashion and beauty. This is a field where the skillful depiction of eroticism can be greatly rewarded. It is an area in which the elements of eroticism become perhaps more intellectual and less visceral than in the ''mens magazines''. In a sense it is somewhat like hearing a joke in response to which you do not laugh but reply''that's funny''. The reason, of course, is that even though the joke does not convulse you with laughter, it does impart an insightful truth with wit. It is this ''conceptual eroticism'' that I find creates a lingering fascination, applauded more by the mind than reacted to on a gut level. »

For twenty five years, through February 1983, all my 35mm images had been made using Nikon equipment. Early in 1983 I switched to the Leica system, with Leitz lenses, which I now use exclusively for my 35mm work. I have found that the quality I get with the Leica is superior to that which I obtained with the Nikon, therefore I made the very expensive switch of systems. Virtually all my photos are made with a Gitzo tripod and an Arca-Swiss Mono-Ball tripod head. Recently I bought the very fine, Elinchrom flash system from Elinca in Switzerland. My metering is done with matched Sekonic meters with Minolta meters standing by. »

PHOTO 1. ''HANDS OF A HAITIAN MASSEUSE''. Nikon F2, 80 - 200 mm Nikkor lens. Daylight. « While at the hotel, Habitation Le Clerc in Haiti, I could not communicate in French with the Haitian masseuse. I asked my neighbor, Miss Beverly Sills, if she would be so kind as to assist me by giving directions, in French. ''Bubbles'' was very kind to oblige. »
PHOTO 2. ''JANICE IN MUSTIQUE''. Nikon F2, 80-200 mm Nikkor lens. Kodachrome 64. Daylight. Photographed for Harpers Bazaar, Italia.
PHOTO 3. ''O.K. SO HE'S GOT SILVER BULLETS''. Nikon F2. 80-200 mm lens. Jumbo Balcar silver umbrella with diffuser. Kodachrome.
PHOTO 4. ''SOMEWHERE BETWEEN VENUS AND THE MILKY WAY''. Los Angeles, California. Nikon F2. 85 mm lens. Milk poured into a black bottom bath tub. Kodachrome.
PHOTO 5. ''ULTRA TAN''. Zurich, Switzerland. Nikon F2, 80-200 mm zoom lens. Kodachrome.

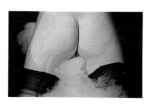

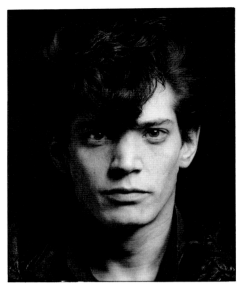

Robert Mapplethorpe has been referred to as the « enfant terrible » of the new wave sexual art scene. Born in 1946, Mapplethorpe was educated at the Pratt Institute from 1963-1970. He is most unique in that he has succeeded in creating extremely erotic photography which has been widely accepted in the art world in addition to working regularly for such high fashion publications as Vogue and others. His work has been the subject of over 36 one-man shows in such galleries as the Light Gallery and Leo Castelli in New York, and top galleries in Amsterdam, Paris, Frankfurt, Berlin, Brussels and Rome. He also has over 40 group shows to his credit in museums such as the Museum of Modern Art and the Whitney Museum of Art in New York, and the Centre Georges Pompidou in Paris, among others. He is the author of the book « Lady Lisa Lyons ». In addition to his work in erotica, he is well known for his images of flowers and portraiture.

ROBERT MAPPLETHORPE

« My pictures were never calculated to shock or outrage. That's never the reason why I take a picture. I took certain pictures because maybe I'd never seen a photograph of a certain kind of sexuality by a photographer who knows composition and lighting. In other words, there was an open territory in sexual imagery because I'd never seen it done by someone who had some kind of sensibility. The people in my pictures are people I know quite well. They weren't doing it for the money, as opposed to working with porno people. They very much wanted something they were doing to be documented. Once I've taken a picture, I'm rather objective about it. I forget that people will be shocked. In fact, I'm always surprised that people are. »

Robert Mapplethorpe works habitually with a Hasselblad, always at F 16, with electronic strobe light, and two umbrellas.

   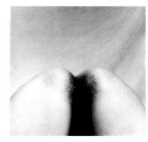 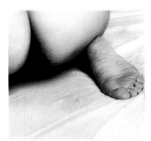 

Ken Marcus began his career in photography in Los Angeles in 1965. Marcus, a native Californian, studied photography at the Art Center School, and at Brooks Institute of Photography in addition to studying with Ansel Adams. In 1974, after several years as a successful advertising and food photographer, he shifted his direction to beauty and glamour. Known for his work in the Playboy calendar and Playboy Magazine, he is perhaps one of America's most published photographers. His workshops and seminars on glamour photography are well attended. He has recently formed a company for the creation of erotic video productions.

KEN MARCUS

« My personal work, with all its simplicity, is the antithesis of my commercially motivated assignments. Simple light, black and white images dealing with essence , not detail. I am interested by body language and musculature and their effect on the viewer. My intent here is not to sell, but to present. Photographic sensuality is subjective; one person's interpretation might not be that of another. Erotic photography has always been of interest. People expressing themselves sensually with their bodies or interacting with another creates visual energy ».

« In selecting the combination of materials for my black and white work, certain criteria came to mind. I require negatives of strong tonality and contrast that can be printed through a mild diffuser. Tri-X rated at 250, processed in undiluted D-76 produced the range of tones I felt were most appropriate. My choice of camera was the Pentax 6 × 7 with the 150 mm lens. This camera permits me to work quickly, like 35 mm, but allows me a negative closer in size to 4 × 5. I prefer not to intimidate my subjects with cumbersome equipment. Most exposures were made with strobe light at F 5.6 with a number 3 diffuser. My only light source was a 4 × 8 ft. softbox with Dyna-Lite strobes. I chose backrounds of painted, unbleached muslin for their texture and detail. »

Before starting his career in New York in 1963, Richard Noble studied as an apprentice with the Horn/Griner Studio. Over the next twelve years he produced many major advertising campaigns. In 1976 he decided to take a sabatical from the photography business and went to live in Ireland where he raised cattle. After six months, he found he missed the work he left behind and began commuting to New York to produce the famous Winston ads known for their sex appeal and

RICHARD NOBLE

direct eye contact. After returning permanently to the U.S. in 1980, he installed himself in a studio in Los Angeles where he now lives and works. His old fashioned photographs from the Virginia Slims ads are world known. Now forty, he is reconciling his need to produce independent creative photography and is moving into more personal work destined for galleries and private collector's. His primary interests are photographing flowers and portraits in addition to erotica.

« When the editors of this book project first approached me about participating, I was thrilled, for it is not every day that one may use sexual suggestions in their images. Most of my work is for American advertising agencies and in most cases the clients choose a more conservative approach to the casting and the attitudes of the people in the images. Once in a while, I can sneak one in, but it's not the norm, so I keep it separate and shoot at night or on week ends when I feel the need to express my visual fantasies. I aim to continue in this direction and find more outlets for the erotic images I create, for I feel they are illustrations of a very strong facet of natural human behavior. »

« Since I can remember, I have always been interested in seeing people touching themselves, or eachother, in an erotic way, of course. A fondle, a kiss, a tickle, a thrill… all of these things, I must admit, are frequently on my mind. At the drop of a hat, my eyes and imagination can conjure up images… One of life's simple pleasures! »

All of Richard Noble's work is made using Hasselblad cameras and lenses. He uses Tri-X 120 and artificial light. His unique tones are a result of a special paper and toning process.

A native of New York, Peter Strongwater completed his education at Boston University and the Columbia University. Before beginning his career in photography, he was an account executive on the Revlon account at Grey Advertising. He then started his fashion and portrait photography which has appeared in such magazines as Vogue, Stern, Newsweek, Cosmopolitan, Penthouse, Gentleman's Quarterly and others. Strongwater has been a contributor to Andy Warhol's Interview since its inception and has photographed many of their most memorable covers and portraits. His current project, «Monuments», Art in America, is a collection of his portraits of Americans who have changed our lives. This project, sponsored by the United States Information Agency, will be exhibited in embassy's worldwide and will be published as a book upon its completion.

PETER STRONGWATER

«In the following pictures I have attempted to convey a feeling of today's female sexuality. The realization that the bondage of the past is the power of today. The models were encouraged to arrange and express themselves as they wanted within the perimeters of the project. No specific directions were given in the hope that in an atmosphere of freedom, as opposed to the usual pre-conceived and manipulated photography sittings of this nature, a newer and truer version of eroticism could emerge. »

All photographs were taken using a Hasselblad camera and the 150 mm. lens. Theatrical hot lights were used for lighting. TXP 120 film was used.

Art Direction : Jeff Dunas.
Color Seperations screened at 160 lines by Rito AG, Zurich, Switzerland.
Duo-tone black and white seperations screened at 175 lines by Berger-Levrault, Nancy, France.
Printed on JOB 175 gram Classic, Brilliant paper in France by Jean-Claude Oger for Berger-Levrault, Nancy, France.
Binding by Diguet-Deny, Breteuil-sur-Iton, France.
The publisher would like to thank Mr. Bernard Lalbat for his generous assistance.